BLACKACRE

Monica Youn

Graywolf Press

This publication is made possible, in part, by the voters of Minnesota through a Minnesota State Arts Board Operating Support grant, thanks to a legislative appropriation from the arts and cultural heritage fund, and through a grant from the Wells Fargo Foundation Minnesota. Significant support has also been provided by Target, the McKnight Foundation, the Amazon Literary Partnership, and other generous contributions from foundations, corporations, and individuals. To these organizations and individuals we offer our heartfelt thanks.

Published by Graywolf Press
250 Third Avenue North, Suite 600
Minneapolis, Minnesota 55401

www.graywolfpress.org

Published in the United States of America

ISBN 978-1-55597-750-4

2 4 6 8 9 7 5 3

Library of Congress Control Number: 2016931136

Cover design: Tyler Comrie

CONTENTS

BLACKACRE

PALINODE

1.

a bird / falls off / a balcony / panicked grasping / fistfuls of / air

2.

I was wrong
please I was
wrong please I
wanted nothing please
I don't want

I

In one hand Nemesis held a designer's square,
or a pair of reins, or an apple branch.

The Marriage of Cadmus and Harmony
(Roberto Calasso, trans. Tim Parks)

INTERROGATION OF THE HANGED MAN

What is your face?
> A house, of sorts.

What is your foot?
> A chipped stone blade.

What did you dream?
> A rain-washed road.

What did it mean?
> It meant nothing.

What have you learned?
> The sky forgives.

What does it forgive?
> Each jet its wake.

What do you want?
> A smile, of sorts.

No, what do you want?
> I want nothing.

What's in your hand?
> A leafless twig.

No. Show me. What's that in your hand?

PORTRAIT OF A HANGED WOMAN

The Greeks
had it wrong:
catastrophe

is not a downturn,
not a fall
from grace.

No, it is
the sudden
terrible

elevation of
a single point—
one dot

on the topography
of a life. That
is the crux

of the punishment:
the singling out,
then that brutal

uplifting.
It is as if
a steel clamp

had seized upon
one square inch
of a flattened

canvas map then
jerked sharply
upward:

the painted landscape
cracking along
unaccustomed

creases, cities
thrown into shadow,
torqued bridges

twisting free.
A life is not
this supple,

it is not meant
to fold, to be
drawn through

a narrow ring.
The Greeks
were wrong.

Necessity
is not a weaver,
there is no spindle

in her hand;
it is a woman
wearing a steel

collar, wearing
a stiffly pleated
dress, which lifts

to reveal nothing
but fabric where
her body used to be.

PORTRAIT OF A HANGED MAN

St. Julian (Piero della Francesca, c. 1470)

the eyes / as if / pinned in / place tacked / up at / the corners / then pulled / taut then

pulled down / then endlessly / pouring down / the unstoppable / torrent from

the unseen / source as / if inexhaustible / downpouring remorseless / but made / of remorse

LAMENTATION OF THE HANGED MAN

The minor winds
hemmed all around

with little brass hooks
of birdsong.

They fasten
on me bonelessly,

failed wings.
They tug at me,

each with its own
pained sense

of imperative.
I am always turning

in the same
idiot arcs,

always facing
the horizon's white-

lipped sneer.
How I would love

to flatten myself
against the ground,

to stop the small
crying blacknesses

of my body with the all-
sufficing blackness

of the earth. Even now
a rake of small-toothed

howls is dragging
toward us, combing out

the hills. If only
I were lying still,

pressed to the ground,
I might be taken

for part of the earth,
tilled into the soil

like any other
enrichment, like labor.

TESTAMENT OF THE HANGED MAN

> ITEM: I devise and leave my body
> *The Testament* (François Villon, 1462)

ITEM: a man
now pendant (still sen-
tient), as tempted, as
amen-

able as Odysseus, strapped to the mast,
seeking knowledge sans
experience: a test
(or a tease)

of the tame,
the sane
meat;
a statement

of intent, of well-meant
amends; an acquiescent an-
athema in its seam-
less unseen net.

◇

ITEM: I bequeath this mean estate
to whoever hungers to taste this marbled meat,
who—having eaten, sated for once—may rest.
This oubliette I once named Little-Ease
now teems with eager tenants: an ants-nest.

EXHIBITION OF THE HANGED MAN

To spectate
is a verb

that does not
mean *to watch.*

It is
intransitive.

Although
the Latin root

spectare
means *to watch;*

nonetheless,
it is wrong

to say
you spectate me;

but not wrong
to say

you watch me.
If you *spectate*

you become
multiple;

you are
an audience

defined by
your attention

to the spectacle.
If I am

the spectacle,
I become

temporal; bounded
in time. I am

an event now,
a kind of show.

I entertain
visitors.

There are
new entrances

to my body,
their edges

outlined in
blacks and grays

and reds like
the entrances

to the face
of a young girl.

MARCH OF THE HANGED MEN

1.

hyperarticulated giant black ants endlessly boiling out of a heaped-up hole in the sand

2.

such a flow of any other thing would mean abundance but these ants replay a tape-loop vision

3.

out of hell the reflexive the implacable the unreasoning rage whose only end is in destruction

4.

the way the dead-eyed Christ in Piero's *Resurrection* will march right over the sleeping soldiers

5.

without pausing or lowering his gaze for he has no regard now for human weakness

6.

since that part of him boiled entirely away leaving only those jointed automatic limbs

7.

that will march forward until those bare immortal feet have pounded a path through the earth

8.

back down to hell because there is no stopping point for what is infinite what cannot be appeased

PORTRAIT OF A HANGED MAN

unremembered
all those years sealed

in the desiccating
chamber what

once fed us now
shrunk to a stark

architecture
sweet segments

long consumed
down to the exposed

core the stripped
stalk the taut neck

stretching up
to that lipless

rictus that almost
unwilling first gasp

fixed in recollection
as if cast in liquid

glass that poured
into you that first time

you let your mouth
fall open that first

second you felt
yourself go slack

PORTRAIT OF A HANGED WOMAN

Now she could see that the air filling their rooms was supersaturated, thick with unspent silences. It was starting to precipitate out, the silences spinning themselves into filaments just below the surface of the visible. They drifted whitely upward like seed floss releasing from summer trees. They clustered together at the darkened ceilings of that house. They made no sound, of course—it would have been contrary to their nature—but sometimes she could feel a small pleased patterning of the air, like a cool current deep underwater. Over time they flourished, doubling and redoubling into braids and garlands, lustrous, self-satisfied. They were long enough now to brush with her fingertips, then to drape around her shoulders—necklaces, scarves. They had the seamlessness of the fur of a healthy animal; she learned to trust in their cohesion, their tensile strength. She knew herself, still, to be a creature bounded by gravity, but now she could travel from room to room never touching the floor. She sensed his approaching footsteps not as sound nor even as vibration but only as a stirring among the coils at her throat.

HANGMAN'S TREE

Yggdrasil

To see a living thing—
a badly damaged
thing—and to fail

to understand
how life still catches
hold of it and clings

without falling through,
like water falling
through a bowl

more fissure than bowl.
Just as a bowl
must be waterproof,

a body must be
lifeproof, we assume,
as if a life were bound

by laws of gravity,
always seeking
a downward escape.

But then there is
this olive tree—
if *tree* is still

the word to describe
this improbable
arrangement

of bark and twig
and leaf—this tree
ripped in three pieces

down to the ground.
No longer a column,
instead a triple

helix of spiraling
bark verticals
sketching the outline

where the tree
used to be. No heartwood,
very little wood

left at all, the exposed
surfaces green
with moss, dandelions

filling the foot-wide
gap at its base. And still
the tree thrives,

taking its place
in the formal allée
that edges this gravel road,

sending out leafy shoots
and unripe olives
in the prescribed shapes

and quantities.
Lizard haven, beetle
home. I was wrong

when I told you
life starts at the center
and radiates outward.

There is another
mode of life, one
that draws sustenance

from the peripheries:
each slim leaf
slots itself

into the green air;
each capillary root
sutures itself

into the soil.
Together these
small adhesions

can bear the much-
diminished weight
of the whole.

I won't lie.
It will hurt.
It will force you

to depend on those
contingent things
you have always

professed to despise.
But it will suffice.
It will keep you alive.

THE HANGED MEN REPRISE

1.

a blunted / hook beneath / the breastbone / as if / someone yanked / out a / strip of /
you a / great inrush / of cold / night and / taillights and / the avenue

2.

the nerves / frenzy feeding / on nothing

3.

I knew / god to / be absolute / zero all / movement slowing / coming to / a stop

II

Trust not an acre early sown,
    Nor praise a son too soon:
Weather rules the acre, wit the son,
    Both are exposed to peril.

The Elder Edda (trans. Paul B. Taylor & W. H. Auden)

DESIDERATUM

But what is it that you want? For example, you are in a high-school parking lot. It's summertime, empty, the asphalt sticky in the heat, or maybe the soles of your shoes are sticking, or both. The humid air is visible—sluggish cellophane ripples, epoxy threatening to go solid. A lone white truck guns its engine. Knotted to its tow hitch, a length of yellow plastic rope, thirty feet maybe, a messy pile. The carbon-monoxide reek. The truck starts up, the yellow rope begins to play out, uncoiling, looping, unlooping itself. Maybe this is a game, a kind of dare—the rope now hissing in widening arcs across the tarmac as the truck zigzags, accelerating, coming around. And you find yourself lurching after it, staggering, then sprinting forward even as your mind is still trying to grasp what that rough plastic rope would do to your hands, what the sudden jerk would do to your shoulder joints, whether, once having grabbed hold, you would ever be able to let go . . .

AGAINST IMAGISM

Late July. The wet
and dry zones of a firefly's
chitinous body

fuse in a blue spark:
a squash-racket-shaped bug
zapper brand-named SHAZAM!

SUNRISE: FOLEY SQUARE

one siren stains the morning in concentric rings

another starts up . . . stops . . . starts again . . . stops—little chips of sound like a climber's
    hammer testing for handholds on an upward sloping face

daylight floods the soundscape with a clear liquid, thickening, flowing over and around [   ]

a lack that could be displaced but not entirely dispersed, an air bubble trapped in rubber tubing

something cone-shaped, nearly discernible, starting to resemble a cry

SELF-PORTRAIT IN A WIRE JACKET

To section off
is to intensify,

to deaden.
Some surfaces

cannot be salvaged.
Leave them

to lose function,
to exist only

as armature,
holding in place

those radiant
squares

of sensation—
the body a dichotomy

of flesh and
blood. Wait here

in the trellised
garden you

are becoming.
Soon you'll know

that the strictures
have themselves

become superfluous,
but at that point

you'll also know
that ungridded

you could
no longer survive.

QUINTA DEL SORDO

Saturn Devouring His Son (Francisco Goya, 1819–1823)

how can I
ask you to

absolve me
my fingers

still greasy
with envy

gaudy oils
still smearing

the dim walls
the quiet

chamber of
my mouth

LANDSCAPE WITH DEODAND

a road
in the trees

from the sound
of it

a milky
shift

in the water
where the silt

shelves down
and the wet

branch beating
for its life

against the pages
of that book

EPIPHYTE

Ficus urostigma

This is an allegory
for what has been discarded

but not dislodged;

what sifts down
from any new avowal—

And already you've paused,
(wary / testing the air).

Your hands trace tentative arcs—
anticipating a familiar

tension, some unseen strand—
but encounter nothing

(no imperative syntax)

(no webbing of ownership / blame).

◇

Because the tree cannot hear,

this cone of sunlight
is all the bugle it knows

(an answering flicker / a flare).

What alternate insistence
could muster itself

against this upward rush,

this eager branch
exposing its throat

(irreproachable)?

It was not your hands
that smoothed

new bark
over the hectic light

(its coruscations / blades and jags).

It was not your hands
that pulled

the grain of the wood
into this simplicity.

◇

As must happen with any
ardor, the outermost

layer of the new branch
hardens into a wall.

Such indifference

does not trouble itself
with seamlessness,

but to find a lapse there—

to find a hold in it—
is not to gain permission,

is not enough.

(Even in this wet air,
it is not enough.)

◇

One green pane
of a leaf drops down,

an ant's detached
antenna—

a seed falls

from a bird's
unappeasable body.

A little twirl of air
guides them down the trunk

as if down a glass staircase

(not to a room)
to a landing,

a crevice
(not a cradle).

◇

Tethered to its perch

(its purchase)

the seed will starve,

will be absorbed into the tree
that is not its parent tree—

(no respite)

it must wrest
its attention

outward and downward,
toward sufficiency.

◇

And the roots go
ribboning down

(prodigious)

and at ground level, a feast
that is inexhaustible,

so that its mode
now shifts

from hunger
to celebration

(the excuse of survival
fallen away).

It is almost unseemly—

this exulting—
the maypole

the seed has made of its body.

◇

And you would claim
a stake in this:

your hands sketch
buttresses, spires

(phrases from the gestural
vocabulary of triumph).

As if your hands
could hasten

the host tree's withering,
the growth of the hollow column.

As if, by sweeping outward,
your hands could draw

(subsistence / substance)

from the horizontals of the ground.
As if these motions

(touching nothing)

were still enough to feed you.

III

The rhizome is an anti-genealogy.

A Thousand Plateaus: Capitalism and Schizophrenia
(Gilles Deleuze & Felix Guattari, trans. Brian Massumi)

GREENACRE

But what if a given surface is coaxed into fruitfulness wrongfully?

For instance, this lushly verdant plain. Imagine it dialed back to featurelessness, each spiraling stalk retracted, each filigree rosette slow-blinking shut. Dialed back to bare promise, to smooth-napped expanse—the forehead of an alien princess might convey such tranquility: she surveys her ranks of suitors, shakes her exquisite green head, in scarcely feigned regret.

So thinks Cadmus—hand still outstretched in a nation-building gesture—as if to freeze in time this instant: scatter of seeds still aloft, arrayed like little dive bombers in formation.

Not yet puncturing the land.
Not yet rooting, not yet sending up terribly thin, ambitious tendrils toward the light.
Not yet trained onto wire-frame espaliers, not yet combed into bombastic pompadours, not yet extruding seed-pods resembling pale grapes, resembling pearls.

The root of "remorse" isn't *tooth*—he recalls, abruptly—but *to bite,* and then stoops, groping for the biggest rock he can find.

BROWNACRE

After the clear plastic sheeting has been pulled back, folded away
After each woody rhizome has been pried loose from the soil
Each snarl of roots traced to its capillary ends
Twigs and pebbles tossed aside, worms reburied elsewhere
After the soil has been rubbed through a sieve
After the ground has been leveled with rakes and stakes and string

No need for further labor, further motion
Nothing has been sown
Nothing is germinating in the raw dirt
The light strikes each granule the same as any other

A windlessness rises
Becomes a precondition

Why is it hard to admit you couldn't live here
No one could live here
This is not the texture of the real, lacking attachment, lacking event
This is neither landscape nor memory; this is parable, a caricature of restraint

But why does this shame you
Even now you're trying to hide that your gaze is drifting upward
This plainness cannot hold your attention
You're searching the sky for some marker of time, of change
In a cloudless sky the sun beats down
But if you observe that the sun warms the soil, you must also concede that the soil will grow colder
The sun stains only the body, and the body is what is simply not at issue here

GOLDACRE

digitize
from the Latin "to finger
or handle" as if

to sink your fingers
deeply

into this
flood of light

◇

hard not to grip
hard not to shape handfuls

loaves
for the hooded basket

something to store away for later
something to place upon the slab

◇

the light
a richer color now

wrong to regret
the reddish undertones of day

wrong to regard them
as a kind of ripening

◇

the young morning
grommeted
with minutes

threaded
with wisps of wool

◇

no signs of resentment
furrow
the infinite

amenability of dawn
no sounds

suggesting discord
from the songbirds

tethered
to their wheels

WHITEACRE

You probably have noticed if you're in a brightly lit room filled with white light, it is difficult to see colored lights. That's because those individual colors get masked by surrounding white light. In the same way, . . . [o]ther sounds will get masked by white noise so they become less detectable. *TM Soft White Noise Player*

Proleptic flinch
of whiteness—

the hunch
of shouldering

into it, stoic
glitch zipping up

its jacket of static—
knit fabric

of interlocking *zs*.
The apotropaic

as abject, self-
replicating reflex

of self-defense.
Vain camouflage

that functions
as neither shield

nor shelter:
the canker's milk

nourishes nothing;
the ice rink

exudes only
its own doom.

45

REDACRE

> "What is it you fear?"
> *Don't Look Now* (Nicolas Roeg, 1973)

couldn't stop / himself picking
his red / lest it

pinken lest / it pale
itself into / mere proudflesh

mere scar / new skin
makes a / smooth mound

hurt hungers / for rebirth
the mouth / that eats

everything then / eats itself / raw

GOLDACRE

We have seen claims that Twinkies . . . aren't baked, the sponge cake instead being "a pure chemical reaction" involving something that "foams up"; the deception is made complete by coloring the confections' bottoms brown to make it appear that they've been baked. . . . As always, the truth is far less exciting than the lore. *Snopes.com*

as if   you were ever wide-eyed enough to believe in urban legends

as if   these plot elements weren't the stalest of clichés: the secret lab, the anaerobic chamber, the gloved hand *ex machina,* the chemical-infused fog

as if   every origin story didn't center on the same sweet myth of a lost wholeness

as if   such longing would seem more palatable if packaged as pure nostalgia

as if   there had once been a moment of unity, smoothly numinous, pellucid

as if   inner and outer were merely phases of the same substance

as if   this whiteness had been your original condition

as if   it hadn't been what was piped into you, what seeped into each vacant cell, each airhole, each pore

as if   you had started out skinless, shameless, blameless, creamy

as if   whipped, passive

as if   extruded, quivering with volatility in a metal mold

as if   a catalyzing vapor triggered a latent reaction

as if   your flesh foamed up, a hydrogenated emulsion consisting mostly of trapped air

as if   though sponge-like, you could remain shelf-stable for decades, part embalming fluid, part rocket fuel, part glue as if   you had been named *twin,* a word for likeness; or *wink,* a word for joke; or *ink,* a word for stain; or *key,* a word for answer

as if   your skin oxidized to its present burnished hue, golden

as if   homemade

REDACRE

Of course Slightly was the first to get his word in. "Wendy lady," he said rapidly, "for you we built this house."

"Oh, say you're pleased," cried Nibs.

"Lovely, darling house," Wendy said, and they were the very words they had hoped she would say.

"And we are your children," cried the twins.

Then all went on their knees, and holding out their arms cried, "O Wendy lady, be our mother."

"Ought I?" Wendy said, all shining. "Of course, it's frightfully fascinating, but you see I am only a little girl. I have no real experience."

Peter and Wendy (J. M. Barrie, 1911)

in a scheme to entice her	they fashioned a shrine	with jewelwork of berries
with crewelwork of vines	red mullions flaunting	flocked velvet drapes
rose patterned carpets	in plush-piled heaps	at the pulsating heart
of this upholstered nest	a snug seat like a socket	that whispered of rest

But I can't be your mother	*I'm not ready yet*	and the eaves of the little home
slumped with regret	and its sorrow turned inward	turned acid turned foul
and corrosion traced stencils	in slime on the wall	and the draperies puddled
in ponds on the floor	and the overripe cushions	ruptured like sores

the seat melted to nothing	a hollowed-out void	drained away everything
in a purgative flood	more taboo than urine	an effluvial flow
streamed toward the sewers	a liquefied *No*	wide-eyed and wide-mouthed
she gaped in dismay	as pearl-like the possibles	went floating away

BLUEACRE

The Passenger (Michelangelo Antonioni, 1975)

1.   The hotel room window is large, seven feet tall by five feet wide, extending down to the floor. It opens inward, two casements with four windowpanes per side. The window opening is nearly a foot deep, painted white, stucco over cinderblock.

2.   A grille of wrought-iron bars protrudes outward from the frame as if to allow for a window box. The bars feature the occasional decorative touch—finial-like ornaments where they intersect, and a scrolled-iron flourish at the sill. The lower bars may once have been a Juliet balcony, but at some point, a second set of bars was clamped on top. The bars of the top half don't line up with the lower half.

3.   The wooden sashes of the casements have been painted a dirty cream, backed by faded, pink foulard curtains.

4.   The window looks out on an old arena—perhaps a bullfighting arena—about a hundred feet away. Yellowish mud bricks with a foundation of rougher, darker beige stone and bricked-in Romanesque archways. A faded red wooden door is visible to the right, with a Moorish-inflected archway, framing a blue round of sky.

5.   Little flakes of birdsong, blunted chisel-strokes.

6.   Between the arena and the window, a motionless expanse of gray-beige dust. The glaring sunlight hits it flatly, as if to subdue it further.

7.   An old man in a gray shirt and pants slouches in a chair against the arena foundations. A small black-and-white dog lies near his feet.

8.   A high-pitched voice—a woman's or a child's—scolds someone in Spanish.

9.   The dog gets up, looks back expectantly at the old man, who fans himself with a newspaper.

10. A man's voice, speaking Spanish.

11. The red door opens, and a man walks out, carrying something bulky over his shoulder, perhaps a folding chair, perhaps an umbrella. He props it against the wall next to the old man. A brief exchange.

12. An engine chugs softly like a toy train.

13.   A rounded, pale-blue car crosses slowly from right to left, not raising the dust. A blue L sticker adheres to its front bumper.

14.   The second man returns to the red doorway and pulls the door shut.

15.   The dog moves left, sniffing the ground.

16.   A shadow to the right, thin as a spear. It is your lover who walks diagonally away from the window, dragging her sandals through the dust. She stops about twenty feet away, looking back. She swivels to face the window, her eyes tautly focused as if in defiance.

17.   A tinny fanfare from a distant trumpet.

18.   Your lover turns, and, with conspicuous slowness, continues walking away, head and arms hanging down.

19.   The little blue car crosses close behind her, the red word ANDALUCIA now visible on its signboard.

20.   Your lover passes out of sight to the far left.

21.   A murmur of far-off voices, metallic as if amplified.

22.   A small boy in a red shirt runs in suddenly from the left, stops in front of the old man. He bends down, picks up something, throws it—toward the old man? toward the dog?

23.   The old man begins berating the boy in Spanish.

24.   The dog emits a single, muffled bark and runs away.

25.   The gravelly rasp of an approaching car, which the boy turns to face.

26.   A lozenge-shaped, pale-green car crosses from left to right and stops abruptly. Only its rear bumper remains visible to the left, bouncing with the suddenness of its braking.

27.   The boy runs off.

28.   Two car doors slam shut.

29.   A black man in a tan suit and a white man in a gray jacket emerge from the green car.

30.   Three muted chimes from a faraway church bell.

31.   The two men look toward the hotel window, confer briefly, arrive at a decision. The man in the tan suit walks toward the hotel, smiling affably. The man in the gray jacket walks off to the left, toward the car.

32.   The swish and slam of a car door opening and shutting in quick succession.

33.   A woman in a red tank top, flounced miniskirt, and red platform sandals suddenly jogs across the square from left to right.

34.   The man in the tan suit, startled, turns to look at her, then continues toward the hotel.

35.   The green car pulls away.

36.   The church bell rings five times, pausing between each knell.

37.   The creak and thud of a wooden door cautiously opening, then shutting. Its latch engages with a gentle click.

38.   The small dog returns to the old man, still sniffing the ground.

39.   A shadow is reflected on the window, subdivided by its panes.

40.   Your lover comes into view back by the arena. She's staring toward the window. She walks, still hesitant, toward the hotel.

41.   Offscreen, the car door opens and shuts again.

42.   The man in the gray jacket reappears and begins walking in a decisive manner toward the hotel.

43.   He pauses to look in the window, raises his right hand in a gesture of acknowledgment, then walks hastily away toward the arena.

44.   He notices your lover and briskly intercepts her, speaking quietly, his words drowned out by an amplified Spanish voice from the arena. He puts his hand on her shoulder and turns her back toward the arena. They walk away together, as he continues talking.

45.   An engine turns over, upshifts to a high-pitched whine.

46.   A muted bang, like a tin box falling to the floor.

47.   Your lover pauses by the arena, and the white man leaves her standing there.

48.   The trumpet, gaining confidence, starts up a long, meandering arabesque in a minor key.

49.   Another drawn-out creak from the wooden door.

50.   The green car pulls into view and drives off to the right.

51.   The door latch clicks firmly.

52.   Your lover is now talking to the old man, with the black-and-white dog sniffing at her ankles.

53.   The sound of a car door opening, then closing.

54.   The old man throws something down in the dust, and the dog begins eating it.

55.   The green car is now driving away on the road around the far side of the arena.

56.   Pausing every few steps, your lover walks away from the arena, then stops short, leaning on one foot, staring toward the window.

57.   A distant police siren, wire-thin, in a swift crescendo.

58.   A woman calls out in Spanish.

59.   The sky now visible above the arena wall.

60.   The camera has moved outside, passing through the bars of the window frame.

GREENACRE

Gold flecked, dark-rimmed, opaque—

    like a toad's
           stolid unsurprise—

    the lake never blinks
             its hazel eye.

Manmade, five feet deep,
the exact square footage of a city block.

    Lakewater murk
           precipitates

    a glinting silt of algae,
            specks of soil,

minnows wheeling in meticulous formation,
the occasional water snake, angry, lost.

    ◇   ◇   ◇

    Two pale figures in the lake,
             half-

    submerged, viewed
            at an oblique angle.

At thirteen, I spent summer afternoons
reading in my treehouse, a simple platform

    without walls,
           like a hunting blind,

    a white painted birdhouse,
           without walls

so no bird ever visited it.
Leaf-light dissolving in still water.

◇   ◇   ◇

Two pale figures in the lake,
                    half-

seen, chest-deep
                    in the mirroring

lakewater so they seemed all bare
shoulders, all lake-slick hair.

          Standing face to face—
                    not embracing,

but his upper arm
                    entering the water,

half-concealed, at an angle that must have meant
he was touching her, beneath the surface.

          Unblinking, the lake
                    giving nothing away,

caring nothing
                    for whatever shape

displaced it, unremembering,
uncurious. Did his arm bend,

          and, if so,
                    to what exact degree?

At what point
                    did his hidden hand

intersect her half-submerged body?
The mirrored horizontal of the lake is where

      memory presses itself
                  against its limit,

      where hypothesis,
                overeager,

rushes to fill the void, to extrapolate
from what is known. Because I knew them both:

      Ann Towson,
              a year ahead of me,

      scrawny, skilled
              at gymnastics, gold

badges emblazoning the sleeve of her green
leotard, her chest as flat as mine.

      And John Hollis—
              the most popular boy

      in our class,
              his tan forearms emerged

gold-dusted from rolled-up shirtsleeves.
He fronted a band called White Minority,

      which played at weekend parties
                  across the lake.

      We shared a bus stop,
              a subdivision.

Once he spoke to me, the day I swapped
my glasses for contact lenses. *Something's different,*

he said, eyes narrowing,
>>Yeah, no kidding!*

I snapped back,
>>turning away. Later,

my best friend scolded me for rudeness.
Every day, boarding the school bus,

>>John Hollis
>>>>faced the bus driver

>>with a bland smirk —
>>>>*What's up, black bitch?*—

as if shoving her face down into a puddle
scummed with humiliation, which was always

>>dripping from her,
>>>>dripping down on her—

>>she hunched her shoulders
>>>>against it, narrow-eyed.

Every day, some kids smirked,
some kids hunched down, stolid, unblinking.

>>◇   ◇   ◇

>>Two pale figures in a lake,
>>>>half-

>>witnessed, half-conjectured,
>>>>a gold arm

like sunlight slanting down through lakewater.
But now a clinging, sedimentary skin

outlines every contour:
                              what is known.

No longer faceless shapes
                              displacing water,

the voids they once inhabited can't be lifted
dripping from the lake, rinsed clean

        enough for use.
                        What drips from them

        coats the lake
                        with a spreading greenness—

an opaque glaze lidding the open eye.

BROWNACRE

We were sitting, leaning back against the house,
on the stone patio, or terrace, looking out over a steep drop

at the mountains arrayed in a semicircle around us,
all expectant angles, like the music stands

of an absent orchestra—summer colors, orangey golds
and dim blues and there must have been greens as well—

I wasn't paying attention: I was watching the thing
you had just said to me still hanging in the air between us,

its surfaces beading up with a shiny liquid like contempt
that might have been seeping from the words themselves

or else condensing from the air, its inscrutable humidity—
the droplets rounding themselves as they fell

etching a darker patch on the patio tiles, a deepening
concavity and, above it, a roughness in the air,

the molecules of concrete coalescing grain by grain
into a corrugated pillar topped by a cloud—a tree form:

not a sapling or a mountain tree, but a tree
that would look at home in a farmyard or meadow,

sheltered from winds, branches stretching out
with all confidence toward the horizon—

a shape that should have been an emblem
of sufficiency, of calm, but whose surfaces

were teeming with a turbulent rush of particles
like the inner workings of a throat exposed and

whose dimensions were expanding with shocking speed,
accumulating mass, accumulating coherence

and righteousness, pulling more and more
of the disintegrating terrace into its form, taller than us,

then shadowing us, and doubtlessly, underground,
a root system of corresponding complexity and spread

was funneling down displaced nothingness
from a hole in the upper air and then it was time

and I stood up and went inside and shut the door,
unsure what still anchored us to the mountainside.

BLUEACRE

Lamentation (Martha Graham, 1930)

What shall I compare to you, that I may comfort you, virgin daughter of Zion? Lamentations 2:13

Wordless, ceaseless,
a second seamless skin—
this blue refrain

sings of comfort,
camouflage, the rarest
right—to remain

faceless, featureless,
the barest rune of ruin:
a chessboard pawn

that rears up into a castle
then topples in defeat,
an exposed vein

on a stretched-out throat
pulsing frantically
as if to drain

unwanted thoughts
into the body's reservoir—
an inky stain

bluer than blushing,
truer than trusting,
the shadow zone

at the core of the flame—
too intense, too airless
to long remain

enveloped, as if
a moth lured to the light
were trapped, sewn

back in its cocoon,
the way the pitiless
mind goes on

shape-making—
gamma, lambda, chi—
a linked chain

of association no less
binding for being silken,
a fine-meshed net thrown

over the exhausted
animal, having given up
its vague, vain

efforts at escape,
and now struggling
merely to sustain

a show of resistance,
to extend a limb toward
extremity, to glean

one glimpse of light,
one gasp of air, then folding
inward, diving down

into the blue pool
at the body's hollow center,
there to float, and drown.

WHITEACRE

the trees all planted in the same month after the same fire

    each as thick around
    as a man's wrist

meticulously spaced grids cutting the sun

    into panels into planks
    and crossbeams of light

an incandescent architecture that is the home that was promised you

    the promise of your new
    purified body

your body rendered glasslike by fire now open to the light

    slicing through you
    through the glass

bones of your hands as you lift the light free of its verticals

    carry it blazing
    through your irradiated life

IV

The Stranger mused for a few seconds; then, speaking in a slightly sing-song voice, as though he repeated an old lesson, he asked, in two Latin hexameters, the following question:

"Who is called Sulva? What road does she walk? Why is the womb barren on one side? Where are the cold marriages?"

That Hideous Strength (C. S. Lewis)

BLACKACRE

one day they showed me a dark moon ringed

with a bright nimbus on a swirling gray screen

they called it my last chance for neverending life

but the next day it was gone it had already

launched itself into the gray sky like an escape

capsule accidentally empty sent spiraling into the

unpeopled galaxies of my trackless gray body

BLACKACRE

Sonnet 19: "On His Blindness" (John Milton, c. 1655)

I.   SPENT

In Sonnet 19, Milton makes the seemingly deliberate choice to avoid "the" and "a"—respectively, the most common and the sixth most common words in English usage. Instead of these articles—definite and indefinite—the poem stages a territorial dispute between possessives: the octave is "my" land, the sestet is "his" land, with the occasional "this" or "that" flagging no-man's-land. We come to understand Milton's mistake—the professed regret of the poem—as this act of claiming. It is only through his taking possession that the universal light is divided up, apportioned into "my light"—a finite commodity that by being subjected to ownership becomes capable of being "spent."

"Spent"—a word like a flapping sack.

My mistake was similar. I came to consider my body—its tug-of-war of tautnesses and slacknesses—to be entirely my own, an appliance for generating various textures and temperatures of friction. Should I have known, then, that by this act of self-claiming, I was cutting myself off from the eternal, the infinite, that I had fashioned myself into a resource that was bounded and, therefore, exhaustible?

The "wide" is always haunted by surprise. In a dark world, the "wide" is the sudden door that opens on unfurling blackness, the void pooling at the bottom of the unlit stairs. To be bounded is our usual condition; to be open is anomalous, even excessive.

A wide-eyed girl is extreme in her unliddedness, her bare membranes flinching at any contact, vulnerable to motes, to smuts, to dryness. A wide-hipped girl extends the splayed arches of her body to bridge the generational divides. A wide-legged girl unseals a portal between persons; she is disturbing to the extent that she is open to all comers, a trapdoor that must be shut for safety's sake. A wide-eyed girl is often thought desirable; a wide-hipped girl is often thought eligible; a wide-legged girl is often thought deplorable. A wide-legged girl is rarely wide-eyed, though she may have started out that way.

We can understand why Milton, in the narrowing orbit of his blindness, would have considered wideness, unboundedness to be threatening. What's less clear is why the wideness of the wide-legged girl is also considered threatening. Does the wideness of the wide-legged girl evoke a kind of blindness, a dark room where one might blunder into strangers, the way two men once met each other in me?

"But why hide it in a hole?" asks the Master, returning from his long absence, smouldering bewilderment sparking into rage.

An unanswered question worries at the Parable of the Talents: why is the Master so terribly angry? It is not as if the servant had stolen the money, or spent it—his sin is one of omission, of overly risk-averse investing. A talent was a unit of weight in ancient Greece: in monetary terms, it was worth eighty pounds of silver, or 6,000 denarii—nearly twenty years wages for the average worker. But Milton uses the word in its more modern sense, dating from the fifteenth century: a natural ability or skill.

How did a word for a deadweight of metal come to mean something inborn, innate? Confusion between the inorganic and the natural trickles into the parable and the poem. The Master prides himself on being a man who reaps where he has not sown and gathers where he did not scatter seed. Was the servant's fault to confuse coins for seeds, did he think he was planting when he was merely burying, did he mistake for viable what had no chance of living, what had never been alive?

4.   BENT

And what about the hole, which for so long had held treasure? Did it wonder why—despite all the moisture and nourishment it could muster—those cold, glinting seeds never sprouted? Did it understand that, if released into the wider world, the coins could have quickened, multiplied? That instead of an incubator, the hole had become an oubliette, a place where otherwise fruitful things were sent to languish, to become lodged, useless?

"Useless"—a word like a capped lead pipe, like the extra bone in my foot I will never pass down to my daughter.

A thing becomes useless if it is bent out of shape. To "get bent" is to be put to another kind of use, a use my therapist considered tantamount to rape. To bend is to be bound, to bow down without breaking, with perhaps just the head tilted at an angle so as to peer upward.

5.   PRESENT

The Master has become the Maker. The servile body wholly "his," splayed wide in a welcome-home, bound up in a beribboned bow.

But the reader will object. This is all wrong. First of all, in the sonnet, "bent" doesn't mean to bow down as if in submission to an outside force, but instead denotes an innate or internalized tendency or inclination. Second, a "present" is not a gift, but a verb meaning to offer openly, full-faced, the sun beaming down on a clean page. Third, the body never comes into it at all.

"Therewith"—a safe word, a strongbox to be buried.

6.   CHIDE

Is a "true account" a story or a sum? Is the Maker an audience or an auditor?

The page scoured white by little grains of fear.

A story has an ending. A sum has a bottom line. There was no accounting for me because my allotment leaked out of me, month after month, I scrubbed the sheets as if effacing the marks of a crime.

Then one day the fear reversed itself. Like a photo negative but in higher contrast—its whites more glaring and its darks more glossy, as if a whisper-thin suspicion had come unzipped.

"Chide" is an enormous understatement. The servant isn't merely scolded, he is cast into "the outer darkness" where there is "weeping and gnashing of teeth." If the "outer darkness" is deemed to be a punishment, then does that lustrous inner darkness count as a reward?

7. DENIED

It seems unfair, is Milton's point. To be assigned a task, but not provided sufficient materials to complete it, is to be placed in a situation of contrived scarcity, like a lab rat or like the youngest sister in a fairy tale.

The Parable of the Wise and Foolish Virgins—which prefaces the Parable of the Talents—centers on this scarcity. The virgins wait for the bridegroom, to greet him with lamps alight. Five virgins have brought extra oil flasks, but five virgins have let their lamps burn out and must go lampless into the night to look for oil. That much we are told, but questions hover around the shadowed margins of the story. Why isn't the bridegroom with the bride? Why is he so delayed? Why is the bridegroom met in the middle of the night by a phalanx of lamp-bearing virgins, like a troupe of pom-pom girls or like a sacrificial rite?

The virginity of the virgins renders them piquant, memorable—much more so, one suspects, than if the parable had called them "maidservants" or even "bridesmaids." Adorning gothic portals, evoking thresholds, entrances, they are a particular feature of French cathedrals.

The presumed desideratum of the story does not interest us much: the sated bridegroom at the midnight feast, the smug, unctuous faces of the wise virgins. Instead, the imagination pursues the foolish virgins rushing into the night, their desperation making them vulnerable, their vulnerability making them erotic, the fill-holes of their useless lamps dark and slick with oil. Is this how I was taught to sexualize insufficiency, the lack that set me wandering night after night, my body too early emptied out?

8.   PREVENT

"Prevent"—a word like a white sheet folded back to cover the mouth.

A white egg bursts from the ovary and falls away, leaving a star-shaped scar. *Corpus albicans,* the whitening body. Such starbursts, at first, are scattered constellations, frost embroidering a dark field. But at what point does this white lacework shift over from intricacy to impossibility, opacity, obstacle—the ice disc clogging the round pond, the grid of proteins baffling the eye?

"Prevent"—a word that slams shut, a portcullis (Latin: *cataracta*).

Letter to Leonard Philaras, September 28, 1654: "the dimness which I experience night and day, seems to incline more to white than to black. . . ."

9.   NEED

Has Patience been looming in the background all along, silent, so as not to intrude upon a blind man's consciousness? Patience, whose garment is "white and close-fitting so that it is not blown about or disturbed by the wind."

At the turn of the sonnet, Patience pries open its sculpted lips, its stiff tongue like a weaver's shuttle drawing woolly strands through the warp and weft of Milton's blindness, a white monologue that admits neither interruption nor rejoinder.

Milton's little murmur stitched back into his mouth.

Woven tight enough to repel need—a liquid beading on the surface, the blood the needles drew from me week after week, hundreds of stoppered vials consigned to the biohazard bin, en route to the incinerator.

"Need," from the High German, for danger.

"Murmur," from the Sanskrit, a crackling fire.

10.   BEST

The best beam in contentment, ranging themselves in rows. Upright as test tubes but forswearing undue pride in such uprightness, mustering shoulder-to-shoulder with the fellow-elect. The best arrayed in regimental ranks, in refrigerated racks, white hymn of the unneeded, white hum of the unneeding.

"Best," originally superlative of *bot* (Old English: remedy, reparation).

The best adopt a pious pose, mouths held taut in tongueless Os. *Sotto voce* chorus of that soft, subjunctive song: *if you were complete . . . if you were replete . . .*

Superlative. The most remediated. The most repaired.

To be scooped out, emptied of need and rinsed clean of its greasy smears, pristine as a petri dish on a stainless lab table. Enucleated, the white of the egg awaiting an unknown yolk.

"Yolk" from *geolu* (Old English: yellow). Not to be confused with "yoke" from *geocian* (Old English: to be joined together). A yoke is an implement, meant to be used, to fill a need. But where there is no field to be plowed, no wagon to be pulled, why demand a yoke that is useless, needless?

One day the Romans sent for Cincinnatus to lead the republic against the invading Aequian army. He laid down his plow in the field and went to war. When the Aequians surrendered, Cincinnatus spared their lives but decreed that they must "pass under the yoke." The Romans fashioned a yoke from three spears, two fixed in the ground, and one tied across the tops of the two verticals. Since the horizontal spear was only a few feet off the ground, the Aequians were made to crouch down like animals in order to complete the surrender. This is thought to be the origin of the word "subjugate," to be brought under the yoke. To bear a yoke is to be bowed down, oxbowed, cowed.

One day they laid me down on a gurney, my feet strapped in stirrups, my legs bent and splayed like the horns of a white bull.

But why would Milton, of all people, use the word "Kingly" as a compliment? Roundheaded Milton, who wrote tract after tract in defense of regicide, who would later be detained for opposing the Restoration?

At this point, our suspicions are confirmed: Milton has disappeared entirely from the poem. We haven't heard from him since the turn of the sonnet. We've been lulled by the cadenced voice of Patience, its dusty tongue self-lubricating, its pallid breath clouding the room, precipitating frangible chains of hydrocarbons, their branchings barbed like fluffs of eiderdown. Through the faint reticulations, we discern no dark stoop-shouldered figure, but only white-robed forms, upright as if hung from hooks, their faces unyielding as lanterns, shuttered as if once aflame.

13.   REST

Rest—a word like a gauze bandage, a ropy weave of collagen knitting its way across a wound. Outspread as if fingered, gelid gestures suggesting solace: to stanch, to shield, to seal, to shut off.

Rest—the rind of the best, a contoured pod that cradles the shape of what it doesn't hold.

Rest—those who are left when thousands have sped away, the bereft, who litter the land, with husks for hands, vacant-eyed, vacant faces raised like basins under the contrail-scarred sky.

14.   WAIT

To stand and wait is a task far weightier than simple waiting. It is to permit the distractible body neither ease nor action, nor food nor drink nor any such reprieve; it is to pit the body in enmity against its own heaviness.

To abide in readiness as in a winter orchard, the lacerated land bandaged in snow. To exist inert as if limbless, skin seamless as if reknit over what had been pruned away, knotted rootstock fit for no other service: no branch, no leaf, no fruit. To persist as a stripped stick persists in a white field, bark peeled back from one exposed split, uptilted as if eager for the grafted slip.

Mercy sugars the starving soil with nitrogen, potassium, phosphate. Mercy captures rain in silver beads and stitches them through the threadbare weave of cloud. Mercy wields a scalpel cutting a cleft in the lopped-off stump, mercy forces home the rootless wand, mercy seals the join with tar and tape.

To foster the raw scion as if it were a son; to siphon light down through its body as if it were your own.

NOTES

The term "Blackacre" is a legal fiction first used by the great English legal scholar Sir Edward Coke in a 1628 treatise. In Anglo-American legal parlance, "Blackacre" is a standard placeholder term used to denote a fictional plot of land, often a bequest, much as the term "John Doe" is used to indicate a fictional or anonymous individual. For example, in a legal hypothetical, one might say that John Doe wishes to bequeath his property Blackacre to his sister Jane Doe. Similarly, one could designate other hypothetical properties Whiteacre, Greenacre, Brownacre, etc. Every law student in the Anglo-American system encounters the term "Blackacre" in his or her core course on property law.

The poems in section I are loosely based on François Villon's 1462 poem *"Ballade des pendus"* ("Ballad of the Hanged Men").

"Greenacre (*Annuit cœptis*)": The Latin motto appears upon the reverse side of the one dollar bill as part of the Great Seal of the United States. In context, it can be translated as: "He favors our undertakings." It may derive from Virgil's appeal to Augustus Caesar in Book I, line 40 of the *Georgics,* which reads *"Da facilem cursum, atque audacibus annue cœptis"* (Give me an easy course, and favor my bold undertakings).

"Blueacre (*Lamentation*)" is formally indebted to Brenda Shaughnessy's poem "Artless."

"Blueacre (*The Passenger*)" is a list of the sounds and actions in the penultimate shot of Antonioni's film, a seven-minute-long, single-take tracking shot in which the camera adopts the perspective of David Locke (Jack Nicholson), and is positioned to look out of his hotel room window.

"Blackacre (*Sonnet 19: "On His Blindness"*)": The description of Patience quoted in section 9 is from Tertullian's *On Patience* (trans. Rudolph Arbesmann). The anecdote of Cincinnatus in section 11 is adapted from Livy's *The History of Rome* (trans. George Baker).

ACKNOWLEDGMENTS

Thanks to the editors of the following magazines, journals and websites where versions of some of these poems first appeared: *The Academy of American Poets: Poem-A-Day*, *The Awl*, *The Bear*, *The Berkeley Poetry Review*, *The Boston Review*, *Folder*, *The Harlequin*, *Horsethief*, *jubilat*, *Lana Turner*, *The New England Review*, *The New Republic*, *The New Yorker*, *The Paris Review*, *Plume*, *Poetry*, *Rattapallax*, and *T: The New York Times Style Magazine*.

"March of the Hanged Men" was reprinted in *The Best American Poetry 2015* (Sherman Alexie, ed., Scribner, 2015), *The Unprofessionals: New American Writing from the Paris Review* (Lorin Stein, ed., Penguin Books, 2015) and, together with "Portrait of a Hanged Man (Piero: St. Julian)" in *Feathers from the Angel's Wing: Poems Inspired by the Paintings of Piero della Francesca* (Dana Prescott, ed., Persea Books, 2016). "Self-Portrait in a Wire Jacket" was republished in *Devouring the Green: Fear of a Human Planet* (ed. Sam Witt, Jaded Ibis Press, 2015). "Portrait of a Hanged Woman" appeared in the *Plume Anthology of Poetry 3* (Daniel Lawless ed., Mad Hat Press, 2015).

Thanks to the institutions where many of these poems were written: Poets House (where I was a poet-in-residence for fall 2015), the Civitella Ranieri Foundation (and especially to Dana Prescott, whose art history talks inspired several of these poems), the MacDowell Colony, the Rockefeller Foundation's Bellagio Center, and the Corporation of Yaddo. Thanks to Josephine Guerrero, Liesl Schillinger, and Mark Wunderlich, for offering sanctuaries where I could write. Thanks to Steve Burt, Drew Daniel, Katy Lederer, Meghan O'Rourke, and Jason Zuzga for their help with the manuscript. Thanks to Jeff Shotts, Katie Dublinski, Fiona McCrae, and all the folks at Graywolf for putting their faith in this book and their efforts behind it. And, finally, thanks to Whitney and Toby Armstrong, for understanding.

MONICA YOUN is the author of two previous collections, *Barter* and *Ignatz,* which was a finalist for the 2010 National Book Award. A former lawyer, she lives in New York and teaches at Princeton University.

The text of *Blackacre* is set in Adobe Garamond. Book design by Rachel Holscher. Composition by Bookmobile Design & Digital Publisher Services, Minneapolis, Minnesota. Manufactured by Versa Press on acid-free, 30 percent postconsumer wastepaper.